The Templer Way

Derek Beavis

OBELISK PUBLICATIONS

OTHER DARTMOOR TITLES FROM OBELISK PUBLICATIONS

Diary of a Dartmoor Walker, Chips Barber
Under Sail through S. Devon & Dartmoor, R. B. Cattell
Diary of a Devonshire Walker, Chips Barber
The Great Little Dartmoor Book, Chips Barber
Dartmoor in Colour, Chips Barber
Dark & Dastardly Dartmoor, Sally & Chips Barber
Ten Family Walks on Dartmoor, Sally & Chips Barber
Weird & Wonderful Dartmoor, Sally & Chips Barber
Tales of the Teign, Judy Chard
The Great Walks of Dartmoor, Terry Bound
The A to Z of Dartmoor Tors, Terry Bound

Dedicated to Mary and Pauline for their patience and support

PLATE ACKNOWLEDGEMENTS
All maps by Sally Barber

Photographs taken or supplied by Chips Barber on pages 4, 7, 8, 11 to 17, 19, 22, 23, 28 (top), 29, 35 to 39, 40 (top), 41, 48 to 50, 53, 55, 57, 59, 60, 62 to 64 and all cover photographs (except front bottom left which is by John Bartlett)

Peter Barrett pp 18, 20, 21, 26 to 28 (bottom), 33, 34, 44; Alan Hutchison pp 40 (bottom), 42, 45 to 47, 61; Tim Hall p 31; Andrew J. Hayes p 58; Chris Jones p 54.

BIBLIOGRAPHY
Devon by S. Baring-Gould MA
Dartmoor by L. A. Harvey & D. St. Leger-Gordon
Haytor Granite Tramway and Stover Canal by Teignbridge DC and DCC (joint report)
Transactions of the Devonshire Association
West Country Railway History by David St. John Thomas
Newton Abbot by Roger Jones

*First published in 1992 by
Obelisk Publications, 2 Church Hill, Pinhoe, Exeter, Devon
Designed by Chips and Sally Barber,
Edited and typeset by Sally Barber
Printed in Great Britain by Penwell Print Ltd, Callington, Cornwall*

The Templer Way

Contents

THE TEMPLER WAY

Introduction

The theme of 'local lad making good' has often been the basis for many of the tales which enthralled us as children. The idea of a poor orphan being raised in the city, running off to sea, making his fortune in a far-off land and returning as a great benefactor, arouses feelings of empathy, even among ardent sceptics. In fact this 'fairy-tale plot' has so often been characterised by many of our great novelists that it has become part of our legendary heritage.

However, the experience of James Templer—born in 1722, brought up an orphan in Exeter, forsaking his apprenticeship as a carpenter, running away to sea and returning as a rich man to purchase a run-down estate within the Bovey Basin—is no fictional story, but a fact of our local history. Showing great sagacity at an early age, he secured a prominent position within the prosperous East-India Shipping Company. On his return to this country he gained contracts which enhanced his fortune, acquired in Madras, and in 1765 he purchased an estate of infertile heathland near Teigngrace. This acquisition included the right for him to quarry the granite on Haytor.

Instead of renovating the ruins of the old Stoford Lodge, which was part of his newly purchased estate, he built a completely new house on a chosen site nearby. Using local Haytor granite in its construction, he erected the house on a hilltop about half a mile away from the old ruins. Not only did James Templer spend much time and money in landscaping the grounds, he also excavated the beautiful Stover Lake, which to this day proves to be a source of pleasure for

locals and visitors alike. This lake was fed from brooks whose origins had been on the high grounds near Ilsington, their flow being diverted into the lake where, at its northern end, an overflow weir drained back into the nearby River Teign.

The nature of James Templer is emphasised on his memorial plaque in Teigngrace Church, where he is reputed to have been a man of great temperance, who was 'never provoked by anything but vice'. However, he didn't live to a great age to enjoy the fruits of his labours; when he died in 1782 he left the inheritance of the estate to his eldest son, also named James. This son had served for thirty years as a Master of the Crown Office, but it seems as if he still shared his father's love for the area and its people, bestowing on the village of Teigngrace its church, erected in 1787.

Teigngrace Church, also constructed with Haytor granite, was originally built with a spire, but this was later removed. Whether James's benevolence was influenced by his brother's chosen career isn't too clear, but it is a fact that his brother John served as the vicar of Teigngrace for some forty-five years. This James was also a shrewd enough businessman to appreciate the increased demands being put upon the clay industry at the time, realising the benefits to be derived from owning a canal to stretch from the area where the clay was mined, to the navigable part of the River Teign. Consequently he excavated the canal from Ventiford to meet up with Whitelake Channel near Newton Abbot, which had originally been dug in order to drain Jetty Marsh. He obviously recognised that such a route would enable him to transport the clay more speedily and efficiently to the waiting ships at Teignmouth.

The clay trade itself had started from humble beginnings, with clay being exported from Teigngrace reportedly as early as 1728. There also exists much evidence to show that clay was later being fairly extensively mined within the Bovey Basin during the 1740s. At that time transport was primitive in that the clay had to be carried from its source to the ships by pack-horse, or at best by means of horse and cart. To make this transportation a little easier, clay cellars were built along the way; one being at Hackney in 1751, where the clay was stored until it could be loaded onto a barge and propelled down the river.

By the year 1770 the demand for clay imposed by the Wedgwood factory and others in the north of the country for feeding the hungry kilns, meant that about four thousand tons were being shipped out of the port annually, this figure rising to between ten and twelve thousand tons by 1793. Therefore, with the backing of an Act of Parliament—the members of which were obviously persuaded on the value of the canal for improving the clay industry—James Templer gained support for his canal. This two-mile stretch of waterway, constructed between 1790 and 1792, was the second canal to be dug in Devonshire — the Exeter Canal between Exeter and Topsham was started in 1563. Although the Act of Parliament allowed for the Stover Canal to extend as far as Heathfield, then on to Bovey Tracey, with a branch line to Chudleigh, it appears as if James Templer—who was the sole financier of the venture— had either run short of funds or changed his mind, for when it reached Ventiford, near Teigngrace, he decided that he had gone far enough. There the canal ended in a terminal basin, lying about thirty feet above sea-level.

The barges which were used to transport the clay were also very basic in design. Being of wooden structure they were about fifty feet long and fourteen feet in width, their only source of power being a single square, wind-propelled sail. This assisted the keel-less vessel to drift up and down the river, depending on the ebb and flow of the tides. Its only other means of navigation was a long pole of some thirty to fifty feet in length, with which the bargeman prevented the craft from fouling up on the river bank. Such a clumsy form of transport was further hampered by the fact that the clay often had to be transshipped in mid-stream; the 'balls of clay' each weighing about thirty five pounds having to be spiked aboard cargo ships. Each barge was capable of carrying some thirty tons, and it was only later, when they were towed in series by tugs, that the tonnage was increased. In its time the volume of river traffic between Teignmouth and the canal was quite extensive, since besides the clay, which was of prime importance, many other commodities were shipped along the route. Coal, mainly for domestic use, and culm—a form of coal-dust used for burning off the locally-quarried limestone—plus timber for the various yards, were only some of the cargoes which needed to be back-freighted from the docks.

Although there were two small local potteries—one at Bovey Tracey and the other at Heathfield—it was mainly due to the absence of locally-mined coal for the kilns that the potteries were never really established here, where the raw material was extracted. The main centre for manufacture thus became Stoke-on-Trent, a fact which had a significant bearing on the development of the port at Teignmouth.

From time to time attempts have been made to utilise what local coal was found—that is lignite—but these experiments have never proved to be much of a success. This is because lignite, like peat and coal, is formed from decayed and compressed vegetation, but unlike coal, lignite does not burn with the same great intensity of heat, therefore it wasn't practical for use in the kilns. However, in periods of extreme scarcity, such as during the years of the war, the venture was again attempted, but quickly abandoned. All this river transportation meant that James Templer was very much involved with the port of Teignmouth, owning at least eight of the ten or more barges which operated from there. Of course he wasn't the only owner, for Kingsteignton also had its clay-producing firms such as Whiteways—established in 1800—plus many local dignitaries like Lord Clifford and Nicholas Watts, who also operated barges from the port.

Revealing James Templer as being a man of considerable foresight, there are reports of how his attention was drawn to a Captain John Schank, who was experimenting with a new form of sliding keel and separate bulkheads on his vessels. In 1791 James Templer was invited to accompany Schank on a voyage from Woolwich to Plymouth in order to witness the tests for himself. It appears as if Templer, having been suitably impressed, was prepared to adopt the idea in the belief that it would enable the coasters from Teignmouth to navigate the river as far as Newton, or even to venture up the actual canal.

However, whether he later decided against the idea or whether the technical details were considered too involved to be overcome, this form of navigation was scrapped as far as the River Teign was concerned.

When James Templer died at the age of sixty five, on the 21st June 1813, his son George inherited the estate, together with the right to extract granite from his quarries on Dartmoor, and he decided to try putting the canal to a further

use. George Templer had secured a contract to supply granite to London where, in 1825, it was used in the rebuilding of such magnificent structures as London Bridge, parts of the British Museum, the National Gallery and the old General Post Office. Consequently he saw potential in the canal being used as the easiest way to get the granite from the moor to London, via Teignmouth. Unfortunately though, the quarries were situated at least six or seven miles away from the canal, up an incline rising over 1,300 feet. In order to establish a link between the two places he created a tramway, constructed from the very same materials it was designed to carry. This granite tramway was opened on the 16th September 1820 amid much pomp and splendour.

Press reports of the time relate how, on the opening day, large numbers of people met at Bovey Tracey, from where they made their way in procession to the site. The account also provides details of the entourage, including everyone from the lowly workman on foot to the horse-riding gentry, and ladies being driven to the site in carriages which were festooned in all manner of trimmings. It was certainly a day of great rejoicing, marking an ambitious venture in which an air of jollity prevailed as George Templer addressed the assembled crowds highlighting the benefits which the scheme would bring to the locality, promising that it would provide more amenities and greater employment. However, his plan was not all that long-lived for, although it was very successful, it eventually proved to be an expensive means of transportation, requiring the granite to be loaded and off-loaded at least three times en route. First, it had to be hoisted on to the wagons at the quarry face, then transferred to the barges at Teigngrace, and from barge to ship at Teignmouth. Therefore, when a rival company devised a cheaper means of obtaining and shipping the granite from other sites on the moor, the Haytor tramway fell into disuse. As a result, after 1858, the Haytor Quarries were only worked for exceptionally large granite blocks for special occasions. One such instance was recorded by E. Amery Adams in *Transactions of the Devonshire Association*, in which he describes how, in 1919, a large block was taken from the main quarry for the Exeter War Memorial.

This loss of occupation resulted in the abandonment of Haytor Village, which had grown up around the works, going into decline as did so many Dartmoor mining settlements before it. Some years later, in 1905, a scheme was proposed for electrifying the line, using lignite to fuel the power-house, opening it up to visitors, but this early idea to promote tourism failed to mature. Fortunately though, we can be grateful that the tramway has since been brought under governmental protection, even though it is only the section on the moor which is classed as a Scheduled Monument. The line consisted of a

single broad-gauge track, laid upon granite rails and fell more than 1,300 feet in its seven mile length. It certainly outlived, and proved to be more durable than, many of the iron rails which were yet to feature in the vast network throughout the country. Certainly the granite track still exists today as proof of the ingenuity of the men who built and worked on it, plus the suitability of the materials used, whereas much of the iron railway system has long since rusted away. Unlike the iron rails which were designed to allow flanged wheels to run along the top of the rail, the granite slabs of between four and eight feet, were so designed as to permit the full rim of the wheel to travel along the base of the groove which was carved into the actual rail. The system carried flat-topped, horse-drawn wagons, linked in series down to the start of the canal at Ventiford, where a crane hauled the blocks from the wagons on to barges. To facilitate the increased traffic, George Templer not only improved the Teign Estuary, he also built the new quay at Teignmouth, again using the granite from his quarries in its construction. As a mark of appreciation, the people of Teignmouth held a public function in his honour on the 10th October 1820, at which about a hundred dignitaries praised his efforts. By early 1821 the New Quay was ready for use, thereby bringing further prosperity to the Port.

Just how successful a businessman he was is left for one to draw one's own conclusions, but it seems as if he might have been a bit of a spendthrift for, in 1829, even though the business was still very profitable, George Templer was forced to sell his estate, together with the tramway and canal, to the Duke of Somerset. Yet, in spite of his apparent faults his abilities must have been highly valued for he was retained as the Granite Company's chief agent in Devon. Whatever his reasons for selling though, his personal affairs must have improved dramatically since, very soon afterwards, he had nearby Sandford Orleigh rebuilt for himself, about a mile away from his old estate. Unfortunately, the granite company itself soon came under difficulties and, when it floundered, the Secretary blamed the problem upon George's inefficiency.

Just how responsible he was isn't clear, but it is certainly true that George Templer was a man with varied interests, being keen on the arts and sports, and reportedly holding lavish parties. Many remembered him for having been the founder of the South Devon Hunt and also for establishing the first cricket club in Devon, while others recall his being a writer of poetry, thereby displaying the many interesting facets of his character. It was his love of sport which led to his being killed in a hunting accident in 1843, thereby ending the family's influence in the community.

Although later, in 1850, it was reported that the granite quarries were again flourishing, by 1858 the trade was eventually lost to the Cornish Coastal Quarries. This firm proved to be more efficient in that the stone could be taken straight to the docks at Plymouth and loaded directly from wagon to ship, rather than needing to go through the intermediary stage on the canal. Even so, in spite of the canal no longer being used to transport granite, the clay trade continued to prosper. Nevertheless, railways were beginning to take over from canals as a more efficient form of transport. Consequently, in 1862 the Stover Canal was bought out by the Moretonhampstead & South Devon Railway. This twelve-mile, broad-gauge line, which climbed steadily upwards rising some 550 feet to Moreton, was opened on 4th July 1866, in spite of the work having been hindered by rising costs and bad weather. Of course, all this was a far cry from later modes of transport, and certainly very much removed from today's high technology. Yet we thrill at the skill and the farsightedness of men like the Templers and their employees who were prepared to wrestle with the elements under such harsh conditions. It is doubtful whether any of those who sweated and strained to move those heavily-laden wagons along the track, contending with all weathers, could for a second have envisaged the ease with which such a task would be accomplished today.

The same could be said of those who spent their lives manhandling the clay. They could hardly have foreseen that the rough material they carried as ugly, shapeless lumps of clay, would one day be in demand for such a wide range of products, from finest porcelain to its use in the manufacture of animal feeds. Therefore, we should regard it as a privilege to retrace their steps, allowing our minds to savour a fraction of what conditions must have been like for those who struggled so hard to survive. As we walk the Templer Way today, we are able to saunter along, appreciating its outstanding beauty, the scenery filling us with a sense of being at one with nature, enabling us to momentarily escape from the stresses of modern living. It is a walk which fluctuates from the wild expanse of Dartmoor, through the wooded areas of Yarner, across open heathland, through the urban areas of Bovey Tracey and Newton Abbot, terminating amid the scenic splendour of the River Teign.

A suggestion might be to start the walk at Haytor in the early morning, arriving at Stover Lake by mid-afternoon, then to leave the remainder of the walk for another time. We might then re-start at Stover Lake in mid-morning, endeavouring to reach Teignmouth for tea-time.

The intention is that eventually the whole route will be linked along as much of the original track as possible. Sometimes, though, much of the tramway has been obscured by modern developments, forcing us to seek alternative routes. Other sections pass over private property, causing more diversions. However, this gives us an opportunity to take advantage of these detours to explore some of the heritage trails en route, such as those existing at Yarner Wood, the Great Plantation and Stover Park.

No matter how we cover the walk, we can be thankful that we are able to retrace so much of the indelible mark which those men inscribed into our local history, leaving us such a comely inheritance. However, because the walk does spread over such a varied terrain, it is best to stress the need to dress accordingly—that is with a good strong pair of boots plus all the gear for serious walking, yet, at the same time trying to keep one's pack as light as possible.

THE QUARRIES ON THE MOOR

Since Dartmoor is notorious for its quickly changing weather conditions, it is advisable to listen carefully to the day's weather forecast before commencing the walk along Templer's Way. Selecting a very fine morning in early summer will lessen the likelihood of being enveloped by the blanket of fog which can suddenly appear as if from nowhere to enshroud the moor.

Because public transport to the moor is so infrequent, it would be best to arrange to get a lift to the car-park at the foot of Haytor Rocks, then to forget about all other means of conveyance, relying only on one's own two feet. Certainly, as any travel guide will be quick to point out, the best way to explore Dartmoor is either on foot or horseback, for only then are we able to seek out, and marvel at, its vast amount of hidden treasures. Past inhabitants of Dartmoor have left many proofs of their existence and, within the area we are

covering in this walk, at least six of the hut circles which abound on the moor are easily accessible. In fact, if we were to venture between Greator Rocks and Hound Tor, we could also explore the site of one of Dartmoor's mediaeval villages. Nevertheless we are likely to find that keeping to this planned walk is sufficiently arduous, and a wise decision would be to leave such investigations for another occasion.

Our eventual destination, Teignmouth, is merely sixteen or seventeen miles away by direct route, but if we are going to take advantage of the full walk we will find ourselves being diverted several times. Therefore our journey is likely to be extended to more than twenty miles, taking about fourteen hours to cover the whole route. We are bound to be tempted to ramble through the various heritage and nature trails en route. Therefore, in order to absorb the full beauty of the changing landscapes, the less ambitious walker, or those who prefer to pause and linger, might find it more practical to

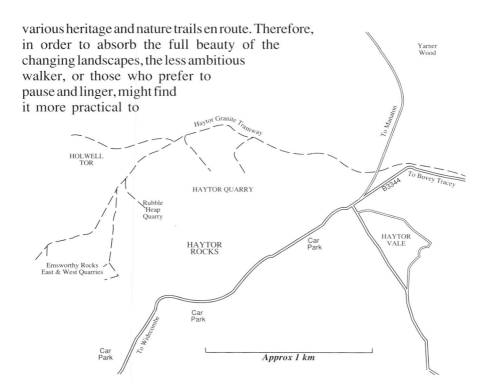

divide the journey into three or four sections. It isn't difficult to trace the granite tramway, since, for most of its length it is very clearly defined as it winds its way to each of the quarries in turn. The same is true as we follow its journey down through Yarner Woods and on to Brimley, but we will need to be a little more vigilant as we approach Teigngrace.

From the car park at Haytor our eyes are bound to be drawn towards the Rock, causing us to marvel at the way nature has provided us with such a

monument, alerting us to the immense forces which once caused the earth's surface to blister and expose such great masses to the elements which eroded it into its present familiar shape. Our exploration of this first part of the moor is confined to the relatively small area of about four hundred acres bordered by Haytor, Hemsworthy Rocks and Holwell Tor. Within this triangle of open moor are the best preserved remains of the quarries from which was hewn granite, considered by locals as being the best in the world. The quarries tell their own story far better than any book, for at the sites themselves, and all along the route of the tramway, are strewn massive boulders which were torn from the rock-face.

Setting out from the car park we walk a short distance back towards Bovey Tracey until just opposite the disused Haytor Service Station we take the small narrow road on the left which leads to Manaton. About fifty yards along we will have no difficulty in picking up the track as it stretches out across the moor, north of Haytor. As we pace along the track, we can notice the effect the weather has had on some of the huge boulders, lying beside the tramway, even splitting some of them completely in two. Yet, in spite of this weathering, the track itself is so clearly visible that it seems as if it could have been constructed within the past few years. In fact, it is still easy to see that some of the slabs bear the drill holes made by the quarrymen.

The length of the granite rails varies between four and eight feet, and would be considered to be narrow gauge in width, being four feet three inches—not so very different from modern railways with their gauge of four feet eight and a half inches.

Tracing the tramway's meandering paths across the moor, we arrive at the first branch line, leading up in a southerly direction towards what was considered to be the main workings. Straddling the moor behind this quarry, forming a huge backdrop, stands the sentinel-like mass of Haytor Rock, while the surrounding slopes are strewn with clitter—a mixture of broken rock fragments of varying sizes and shapes. The word clitter is thought to have been derived from either the Welsh 'clegyr' meaning simply rock, or the Cornish 'clegar' indicating a sort of avalanche of masses of rock. Whichever is the better definition isn't clear, but the baffling question regarding clitter is to understand why it happens to be in its present position. It usually lies farther distant from the foot of the tor than might be expected and, although it is fairly obvious that this particular mound originated from Haytor, we could be forgiven for thinking it ought to lie nearer to the tor itself. One explanation offered by experts is that such clitter broke away and fell mainly during periods of glacial activity when the ground was supposedly covered in several feet of ice and snow. Under such conditions it is thought that the boulders would slide along the ice-covered surface, coming to rest some distance away. However, other sources tell us that Dartmoor was not affected during the British Ice Age, and that the clitter broke away from the parent rock through the action of frost and cold, but if this is so then its distance from the tor remains a mystery.

Whatever the explanation, back on the track a more pertinent puzzle confronts us, that of the well-preserved specimens of switch-work, located at each intersection. Normally, on modern railway systems, the points designed to switch trains from one line to another are operated either mechanically or

manually by a lever pulling the two lines together, or separating them from one another. However, on the granite tramway no such system is apparent, and it is difficult to assess how the branch lines merged into the main route. It is possible that the track was laid in such a manner that the force pulling the train was sufficient to pull the vehicles through the gaps left between the slabs at these crossings, then along the track in the desired direction. On the other hand, it is noticeable that at almost every intersection can be seen a drill hole, suggesting that a rod of some description might have been inserted in order to temporarily make the line whole.

As we approach nearer to the first site, Haytor Quarry, we see that even though parts of the route have been eroded by the weather, it is still reasonably easy to follow, right up to the quarry face. By walking up the incline on the left side and entering through a gate which remains unlocked, we will find that the

visitor is allowed to explore the site. From here we are also able to peer down into the crater which constituted the first work area and behind this lies the main quarry. Once inside this site we see many signs indicating the nature of the work which was performed. Lying on its side is a large timber beam, together with its discarded winching gear, and a little distance from these can be seen iron rings, embedded into the rock, which anchored the hoist. Our imagination need not be taxed too far as we realise how this machinery formed part of the crane with which the blocks were hoisted on to the wagons.

This disused site, now partly flooded, has become an adventure playground for groups of supervised children who visit the moor as part of their school curriculum. This was the case with the group we met up with, who, accompanied by their teacher from Barton School in Torquay, were spending a week on the moor. Who could blame them if their attention was more drawn to catching tadpoles and newts in the pond, rather than being enthralled at the samples of 'feather and tare' methods of splitting the rock. These samples which can be seen on the eastern part of the quarry remind us that this method was employed all over the moor after 1800. On particularly dry periods we can also see that more iron-work and other remains of the industry lie submerged beneath the waters.

The atmosphere inside the quarry enables us to appreciate what life must have been like during the days when the moor resounded with the shouts of men gouging out the rock, mingled with the sound and smell of the horses being harnessed up to their loads, and no doubt we will be loath to leave the site too readily. Retracing our steps back to the intersection along the track, we are bound to be aware of the abundance of wild life we can expect to encounter on our trip. In recent years there have been numerous reports of sheep being attacked and mauled in an unusual way, giving rise to rumours of ferocious animals, presumably of the cat family, inhabiting the moor. Time

alone will reveal whether or not there is any truth in such scares, but the writer and novelist, S. Baring Gould stated that he and his brother killed what was most likely the last wildcat, at Lew Trenchard in 1852. Nowadays we would consider ourselves fortunate if we caught sight of a fox or badger, even though both animals make their home here.

Rabbits and foxes are still fairly numerous, although we are not likely to find

such large numbers as existed before the introduction of myxomatosis. Foxes, who find an ideal home on the clitter, feed off rabbits, field-mice and beetles, and it is estimated that three or four can be found occupying every square mile of moorland territory, this figure rising to as many as ten per square mile in the early spring, each pair usually producing four to six cubs.

Hares, on the other hand, although they do inhabit the moor, are usually in such small numbers that it is unlikely for the casual visitor to ever set eyes upon them. Of course these different forms of game entice many predators, and a faint rustling in the undergrowth could indicate to the more stealthful of us the presence of a stoat or weasel. Sometimes a badger might even dig its sett in the clitter, but this is the exception rather than the rule, for the soil here is most often too acidic or waterlogged. Whether or not we are fortunate enough to catch sight of such animals, even the casual rambler is bound to be delighted by the presence of domestic creatures—the ponies, sheep and cattle which, because they roam free, are considered to be wild. However, all these animals belong to farmers or homesteaders who exercise grazing rights acquired early in our history. Generations of ponies have roamed here, in relative freedom, with a cull taking place annually; the result being that many of their ancestors have ended their lives as pit ponies, or the more fortunate among them might have become a child's first riding pony.

Although sheep have also grazed the moor from time immemorial, it was not until early in this present century that the area became primarily a good sheep range. A hundred years ago the big flocks we now see were unknown, the change coming around 1910 with the introduction of the Black-faced Scotch Sheep, introduced to improve the strain of the local Dartmoor breed. Even so, in spite of popular belief, these flocks still require careful management, particularly during the winter months when feed is scarce. Today we are likely to come across many of the four breeds: the Whitefaced Dartmoor, the Grey-faced Dartmoor (or Improved Dartmoor), the Cheviot Sheep or the Black-faced Scotch.

At one time we most likely would also have seen deer roaming the moor, but the last indigenous Dartmoor deer was killed in 1780. There have been a few attempts to re-introduce them, but it is rarely that the visitor can expect to espy them during the day, even though many residents often lay claim to have encountered them, particularly at dusk. It is believed that any we might see are likely to be stragglers from Exmoor or the Dartmoor borderlands.

Other animals we are certain to meet on our walk will be the scattered herds of cattle belonging to farmers living on the edge of the moor. Although we are not likely to find any of the brown, smooth-coated South Devon breed roaming free, we are bound to encounter the more hardy Galloways and Hereford crossbreeds, and we might be fortunate to meet up with a few Highland cattle, with their shaggy coats and long horns,

blending into the landscape; these however, are mostly confined to the western side of the moor.

Having fully explored Haytor Quarry, we make our way back along the main tramway as it winds its way deeper into the moor. Resisting the urge to follow the more pronounced track which leads off to the north-west, we are diverted to a further quarry on the left. To arrive at the face we have to trace the route through a type of ravine, almost due north of Haytor Rock. Actually, there is only one cutting, or embankment, on the tramway, but even though it is obvious where this track led, it is less clearly marked than some of the others.

As the ravine opens up into a wide space in front of this quarry, we need to exercise caution for the ground here can be very swampy, and we must also appreciate the need to be particularly mindful that this can be a favourite spot for adders to be basking in the sunshine, and we certainly wouldn't want to disturb one accidentally. There are also harmless reptiles to be found here such as slow-worms, grass-snakes and common lizards.

Upon retracing our steps back along the cutting, we might pay attention to how the smaller pieces of granite were built into the walls forming the embankment, and we might also notice the rubble heaps where the rocks, considered to be unworthy of further attention, were dumped. Walking back through the gully, the unique atmosphere of Dartmoor begins to overwhelm us. On the still air, the voices of other travellers reaches us from quite a considerable distance, amazing us at the wonderful acoustics, unhindered by any background noises. This fact helps us to understand how speakers of times past were able to address large crowds from amphitheatres without resorting to modern electronics of microphones and amplifiers.

As we pass the ruins of houses which were once inhabited by the quarrymen and their families, we envisage what life must have been like in this vast desolate space, which is inclined to play tricks on one's sound and vision. It is easy to appreciate how much of the folklore attributed to Dartmoor originated, particularly if one is caught up in a mist. Many travellers have mentioned how the barren expanse emits an eerie feeling of one's being watched the whole time. Because of such loneliness, it is also easy to understand why, when the quarries were abandoned, the occupants of the houses soon moved into

cottages adjoining the Rock Hotel.

Returning to the main track, we might hear the call of the cuckoo, from a nearby wood, causing us to speculate whether, like so many of its predecessors it began its life in the nest of a couple of unsuspecting meadow-pipits. Skylarks and meadow-pipits are just about the most common breeding birds to be found here in early summer, but stonechats and winchats are also relatively common. Wrens too are numerous as are wheat-ears, who find interesting nest sites among the crevices of the rocks. These latter are quickly recognisable by the flash of white from their tail feathers as they make their short brisk flights in among the bracken and gorse; their clacking calls warning one another of our approach. Among the birds of prey we might encounter on our walk, the buzzard is perhaps the most majestic, although we could even be fortunate enough to see a falcon making a headlong swoop on some hapless victim. More likely we will catch sight of harriers in the wooded or coppiced areas, while ravens, carrion crows, jackdaws and magpies are everywhere scavenging an existence, feeding off the carcasses of dead animals wherever possible. Kestrels too are known to use the ledges of a disused quarry as a suitable nesting site, except for when they 'squat' in a discarded magpie or crow's nest, thriving on the voles, shrews and long-tailed field mice which are abundant.

The main route now begins to peter out as we head towards Holwell Tor and it becomes more difficult to follow as the tracks appear to criss-cross in all directions, in most cases disappearing altogether. Just as we think we have picked up the route and are encouraged to continue, we just as quickly lose it again. Obviously this was an area of much activity, but possibly the exact route has now been lost for all time. Maybe we might consider this as an opportune time to sit for a while on Holwell Tor, enjoying the quietness and the breathtaking panoramic views which stretch out before us. When rested we

head back along the track to investigate the remaining quarry on the north side, Holwell Quarry. This lies at the bottom of a steep slope, the gradient of which makes us aware of just what was involved in transporting those heavily laden wagons over such hostile ground.

The trucks used had very little in common with modern railway wagons, being about thirteen feet in length, with a wheel-base of ten feet, they more resembled road-drays, with a flat base supported on a chassis. Each truck was capable of carrying two or three blocks at a time. Linked together in series the leading truck was furnished with shafts, and the whole train was then harnessed to a team of anything up to eighteen horses.

During our trip, on a pleasant summer's day, we might harbour romantic impressions of those noble workers, decked out in corded trousers tucked neatly into leggings and worn over a stout pair of boots. No doubt such an imaginative picture is reminiscent of Gray's ploughman plodding his weary way homeward, gently leading the heavy, blinkered beast along the track. However, nothing could be further from reality, for it must be remembered that work on the tramway was performed throughout the whole year, and in all weathers.

A more realistic view would be to realise how the moor often resounded to the men's curses as they belaboured the poor beasts under their charge, persuading them to ply their strength in getting the wagons rolling. No doubt the work had its dangers, and we can imagine how harrowing it must have been as they applied the brakes to prevent the trucks from tumbling down over the slopes. Reflecting on such scenes, we might envision that we can even yet hear the sound of the clumping hooves on the hard turf, or the mud squelching beneath them in winter, all harmonising with the jingle of the harnesses and the clanking of chains.

There are many interesting relics to see at Holwell Quarry, for not only is the track itself very clearly marked, but so are the side turnings where the trucks were stored, and further mounds of rubble were discarded. We can also explore the remains of buildings which housed the workers and their equipment, and at the far end of the quarry is a well preserved shelter. This small, igloo-shaped building was probably used as a store for tools, or maybe as a shelter from blasting. Taking a look inside, we might be surprised to see how the roof is constructed from just two granite slabs, overlain with smaller stones and rubble. Making our way back up the incline, we again

appreciate how the haul from here must have really tested the strength and endurance of both men and beasts, for the gradient rises from 1,100 feet above sea-level to 1,275 feet in half a mile. Yet, arriving back at the Manaton Road, we are bound to feel that this first part of the trip has been worthwhile. It may also be sufficient for one day, but if we have the stamina to continue the next leg of the journey, then we will certainly find it to be equally as interesting.

THROUGH YARNER WOOD TO BRIMLEY

Having thoroughly enjoyed our expedition around the quarries north of Haytor Rock, we are now eager to progress further along the route as it leads down towards Stover.

On this eastern edge of the moor, the tramway passes by one further quarry before plunging down through Yarner Wood. We will find that the journey through Yarner contains a wide variety of flora and fauna, with attempts having been made to manage the woods systematically with particular attention being given to the different areas playing their individual parts in the provision of the food chain. This second section of the walk actually starts at

the same stretch of road, opposite Haytor Service Station, where we commenced our first trip. From here, turn eastward and follow what remains of the track as it runs parallel with the Bovey Tracey road.

Once again we are bound to be impressed with the glorious view, as we see the entire route stretching out before us with the river's finger of light blue water beckoning us towards Teignmouth.

As we notice the clay-pits at Teigngrace and Kingsteignton, we are aware of how material from this area was exported to all parts of the world for use in many of the commodities we use today. Looking down on this scene, we automatically reflect on what this sight must have meant for those men who were leading their heavily laden teams down through this incline to Teigngrace. What impression did it make on them as they caught sight of their goal? Were they inspired to put a greater spring into their step, or were their working conditions so extreme that they thought of nothing more than completing their assignment as quickly and as safely as possible?

Today we are fortunate in being able to adopt a leisurely approach, allowing our minds to drift back across a century and a half of time, dispelling the thoughts of the hum-drum existence experienced by such workers. During its hey-day, up to a hundred men at a time were employed in various capacities on the tramway or at the quarries, and we can be grateful for this opportunity of visiting this living memorial to their expertise and the way they inadvertently enhanced the countenance of the moor. Even so, we can only expect our excursion to reveal the merest glimpse of their skills, emphasising their struggle to wrest from nature's grasp the materials needed for the construction of buildings which, in turn, became symbols of other men's achievements.

An Old View of the Moorlands Hotel, Haytor

Before starting this part of the walk, we might give a thought to the type of plant and insect life we can expect to encounter en route, noticing how it compares with that found on the higher moor. Since this area is more remote and undisturbed by the vast amount of tourists, we would be advised to pause frequently to absorb the atmosphere and acquaint ourselves with some species which have been undisturbed for centuries, rather than pacing out to cover as much ground in as short a time possible.

To many people who make the occasional trip, Dartmoor is regarded as a vast barren waste, clothed in yellow gorse and purple heather. It is rarely that they appreciate that besides the two more common species of heather, there exists a wide variety of smaller plants, all struggling for existence. These include many low-growing plants, such as mosses, liverworts and lichens, and it is the whole profusion of colour from the growth in between the heathers which adds to the overall beauty of the moor. Feeding off these plants are the many species of butterflies and moths which have been disturbed by our presence, among which we will no doubt recognise meadow-browns, gatekeepers, small-heath, small-copper and common-blues, while early in the year we might also catch sight of fox-moths or emperor-moths. Grasshoppers of many kinds also are to be found here in large numbers, as are a variety of wasps, bees and many insects we might never have seen before.

Unfortunately, at this lower edge of the moor, much of the track has been effaced, not only by the elements but also by the trampling of men and animals. Consequently, since the route has been obscured in so many places, we will need to be more diligent in our search. However, as we walk parallel with the tarmac road, just opposite the Bel Alp Hotel, our efforts are rewarded by finding what is obviously part of the track, beside which is the first milestone, bearing the number '6' informing us that we are six miles from our destination

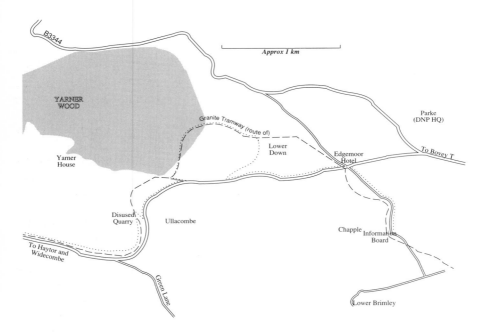

at Teigngrace. From here we notice that the route begins to veer away from the road, turning back again on to the moor itself. The remains of the tramway become clearer from here and by keeping to it we will soon find ourselves at the last quarry on the moor.

This is a relatively small work-face, with quite a wide open space at the foot. We will notice here that the track actually ran past this quarry and down across open ground towards Yarner Wood, but this now crosses the private property of Long Brake Farm. Therefore, in order to get back on the route, we will need to make our way down through the bridlepath to the main Bovey Tracey road.

However, before leaving this quarry, there are a few things to interest us, for even though there are not many visible signs of its links with the tramway, we can be certain that it played equally as important a part as the others.

Unfortunately, when we visited the site, we discovered many indications of the open space in front of the quarry as having been used for more nefarious activities. Laid out in front of the quarry were many small stones, formed into patterns as might be used by those who practise the occult. This, together with the remains of fires, causes one to wonder whether such misuse is worthy of further investigation.

Going away from the tramway for a moment, and passing by the quarry along the moorland track, we will notice many signs of where badgers and other animals have been burrowing. This isn't surprising for it is a remote part of the moor with a sinister atmosphere where many ancient trackways criss-cross.

However, to get back to our walk, we progress along the bridlepath down to the main road, over the cattle grid and continue along the metal road towards Yarner. Here we need to be extremely careful for the road is unpaved and the traffic to and from the moor is fairly heavy. As we turn into the private road towards Yarner, about a hundred yards along on the right hand side, we pick up the tramway once again; it runs along the road towards us, enters a gateway and temporarily disappears across a field. A few yards nearer towards Yarner, we see a more clearly defined track, but since this is a private road we are not allowed to progress further. Instead, just beside Yarner Lodge we find that an alternative route has been designated through the woods. These Templer Way signs direct us through a kissing gate and along a clearly defined trail, but we need to take note of the warning to show respect to this Nature Reserve. It is imperative to keep all dogs on a lead and to ensure that unless we have gained permission we must only keep to the planned Templer Way.

If we wish to walk the Nature Trails through the reserve, then we should contact the wardens, access to the woods being along the B.3344 towards Becka Falls, turning into the car park. It would be a pity to miss out on adding to our trip the pleasure derived from following the Nature Trail, picking up the tramway again after enjoying the delights of this Nature Reserve which was established in 1952. Since that time much work has been done to bring the woods under proper management; the objective being to retain the woods in as natural a state as possible and to encourage the wild life to make the wood their natural habitat again. For this reason much emphasis is put on keeping to the prescribed routes, in order not to disturb anything more than necessary. To accomplish this objective, many of the trees and plants, considered to be foreigners which have come in and choked the native oaks, ash and hazel, have had to be controlled.

The official walk through the woods, which is about three miles long, will doubtless appeal to the historian of whatever persuasion, for besides containing a small museum, it includes passing the ruins of a copper mine whose history extends back at least to 1858. Records tell us that in 1862 this mine was three hundred feet deep and employed fifty people, and by 1865 had produced 2,300 tons of copper. There are many such mines around Dartmoor, but it seems that during the 1870s copper-mining was no longer profitable, thus most mines were abandoned. Therefore its existence at this location is no surprise since much of the oak was used for charcoal burning, and the charcoal thus produced was used in smelting the ore.

A note of caution needs to be expressed at this point, for even if we had sought permission to walk the nature trails, it certainly is not advisable for anyone to approach the mine without supervision. The ruins are extremely dangerous, hence the reason for their being fenced off from the public. Although the main shaft, which lies below the engine house, was filled in when the work ceased, this infill has since collapsed, leaving a deep crater. Also to be found within this vicinity are the heaps of waste rock from which the copper was extracted with water-powered hammers. This waste contains traces of arsenic, a mineral which is found with tin and copper; although when originally working the mine this product was discarded, it eventually proved to be more profitable than the copper, but the work in its production was extremely risky.

However, to resume our walk, we will find that as we enter the wood from near Yarner Lodge, this area is not quite so densely populated as others. In fact, this part of the wood provides shelter against the winds coming direct from the moor, attracting a considerable amount of sunshine, which in turn encourages a wide variety of insects with attendant predators.

Only a relatively small section of the tramway actually runs through the wood, but it is perhaps the best defined of all. In the wood was a further quarry but this is now so overgrown that we would need to search intently for signs of its existence. However, on the bank on the right, we can see another well-preserved milestone, this particular post indicating that we are yet five miles from the canal. Our walk through the wood passes by a variety of trees, including oaks, birches and beech, plus a selection of pines, all having gone through stages of management. Being a mixed wood, safe nesting sites are provided for birds of all kinds, ranging from sparrow-hawks and buzzards to nuthatches, treecreepers and coal-tits and we are almost certain to espy the quick flash of a woodpecker or two.

Our ears will also be strained to catch the sounds of the more elusive song-birds, and we are sure to discern the harsh call of jays.

If we had decided to cover the Nature Trail we would have found that many streams run through the wood, including Bovey Pottery Leat, which was constructed about 1859 for feeding the potteries with water from Becky Falls. This area is one where we can watch for signs of badgers who, although they seldom let themselves be seen, leave much evidence of the presence of their setts.

Whether we explore the nature-trails, or just keep to the Templer Way, due to the fact that most of the track covers land which has since been developed by private ownership, we will only be able to follow the tramway through the woods for a further five hundred yards before we find ourselves diverted back on to the main Bovey Tracey road. This means travelling along a pathway around the borders of a field which is very steep and muddy. Emerging from this path at Bradnick Hill, a quick glance up the road shows that the distance we have travelled is a mere two hundred yards from the entrance to Yarner even though the journey through Yarner has added another mile and a half,

perhaps four or five if we took the Nature Trails, yet we are bound to feel justly rewarded by the experience.

Meanwhile, the tramway actually crosses fields down to the road which runs beside the Edgemoor Hotel, leaving us no alternative but to travel along the main road down to this point. However, it cannot be over-emphasised just how important it is to recognise the dangers on this unpaved road, and the need for walking in single file.

Unfortunately, even though a few setts from the tramway lie scattered on the lawn of the Edgemoor, it is no longer possible to discern exactly where it crossed in front of the hotel, but opposite the entrance we notice about twenty yards further, a sign for a bridlepath to Whissel-well Farm. Here, the tramway

enters the private wood and travels down through the wood, emerging onto and running along Chapple Road. The No '4' mile stone used to be at this spot.

The track through the wood and along Chapple Road is very clear to where it crosses the Bovey Leat, over its only surviving bridge. If we had not been aware that this was part of the tramway, we could easily have assumed it was a raised pavement, with somewhat unusual kerbstones. The information-board sited at this bridge explains that in 1957 the potteries finally closed at Bovey and, due to the high cost of maintenance, the greater part of the leat was abandoned. But here, as it crosses Chapple Road, it is in a very good state of preservation.

Tracing the remainder of the track will not prove difficult as it runs along a small pathway, just behind the road, until it re-emerges and crosses the road, leading down another bridlepath on the left hand side.

This pathway is actually also part of the tramway and has been allowed to remain in the same condition as at its start, not suffering through modern farming techniques. In fact, it is so quiet and peaceful along this track that it is easy to forget that less than fifty yards away modern houses back on to it. As we progress along the route we again experience the sensation of having stepped back through the pages of history. The only thing marring such an illusion is in the way people have obviously been using the route as an exercise ground for their dogs! The track eventually emerges into Brimley Road, crosses Ashburton Road, finally spilling out behind a row of houses along Pottery Road. However, between Ashburton Road and Pottery Road we need to watch out for milestone No '3' on the left side of the track.

The remaining three miles into Teigngrace have now been altered extensively, obliterating all signs of the tramway and we are faced with the choice of either searching for the few remaining evidences of its existence, or availing ourselves of the more pleasurable route which has been forged through the Great Plantation.

Those of us who opt for keeping as close as possible to the original course will have to make their own way, since there is no signposted route, but before venturing further, those interested in social history will doubtless want to explore the remains of the eighteenth century potteries. Most of the site has now been divided into small industrial units, but from the rear of these buildings we can see the remains of kilns and furnaces— however it must be borne in mind not  to trespass on private property without permission. Sadly, most of the other artifacts are fast disappearing, as is the case with the weighbridge, near Pottery Road, which was, in 1991, in the process of being removed.

Time spent at the site of the potteries will certainly be worth the effort, stimulating us to discover more of the history of the industry before we decide which of the routes to follow into Stover Park.

BRIMLEY THROUGH STOVER COUNTRY PARK

In order to try tracing the line of the tramway, we need to progress along Pottery Road towards the roundabout at Pottery Bridge. Unfortunately though, since it is not permissible to walk the original route along the railway line to where the canal met up with the canal at Ventiford, we have to compromise.

Before the Bovey Tracey by-pass was built some evidence of the tramway could still be traced to a granite siding on the railway, but this has now been lost. All that remains is the overgrown piece of waste adjoining the cottages at the bottom of Pottery Road. British Rail still own most of the land over which the track ran, so we are naturally prevented from following the exact course into Ventiford but it will still interest us to know of its location.

The nearest we can get to the line of the tramway is to go across the roundabout from Pottery Road, to the old Bovey Tracey Road where, just before the turn for the old Newton Road, we see a small lane on the left, previously known as Accommodation Lane, but in more recent times referred to by locals as Piggery Lane. This was part of the original route, which a little further on was later incorporated into the railway track. Unfortunately this very muddy track runs across private land, for which permission will have to be sought for access, but a little knowledge of the railway's history will help us to understand how the route was lost.

In 1861, when the Moretonhampstead and South Devon Railway was established, it was charged with the responsibility of constructing the line from Newton Abbot, through Bovey Tracey and on to Moretonhampstead. Thus it seemed more than providential that the following year, when the Duke of Somerset agreed to sell the lower part of the tramway together with the canal, that they should purchase the tramway, which had really ceased functioning by 1858, for £8,000. Part of the existing track was then utilised as a base upon which to lay the railway line.

At that time, the canal was still operational—even though the clay industry was its main and practically its sole customer—therefore the railway company, somewhat reluctantly, agreed to incorporate this service within its own operation. Even then, when the line met up with the canal at Ventiford, the company saw wisdom in running the line parallel with the canal into Newton Abbot.

As previously mentioned, this broad-gauge railway track which opened in 1866, climbed 550 feet between Newton Abbot and Moretonhampstead. Originally there was only limited support for the venture, but it struggled on until 1872 when it was taken over by the larger South Devon Railway Company. Later, in 1877, the Great Western replaced the South Devon Railway, including its interests in the canal, but even then railway traffic remained somewhat sparse until the end of the century.

This is an aerial view showing the Candy Tiles Works and surrounding area. On the right is Heathfield Station ("Chudleigh Road"). The Moretonhampstead line can be seen going towards the top of the photo whilst the Teign Valley Branch line curves away to the right. The A38, long before it was a dual carriageway, goes along the bottom.

Although at first the railways showed little interest in freighting the clay, agreements were reached whereby they should continue to be responsible for the canal's maintenance for the benefit of the clay traders. However, in spite of pressure, they would not obligate themselves to maintain the stretch of canal above Teignbridge Crossing. This was not as churlish as it might at first seem, for it was only the lower part of the canal which was used by the clay companies. Actually, by the time it came under the control of the Great Western in 1877, Watts Blake & Company were the sole lessees of the canal, therefore, when their lease expired in 1942, the Great Western released themselves from any further liability of maintenance.

Because the railway company laid their line on the actual bed of the tramway, any remaining proofs of its existence here is fragmentary, most having been discarded long ago, including the only iron rails used on the whole system which carried the track over a small gully near the siding at Pottery Bridge.

For a few years after the 1939–45 war, the line flourished due to the redevelopment of the lignite industry at Heathfield, but as with previous attempts to mine this product, the project proved to be unsuccessful, and from then on the line was used only infrequently. Parts of it are still operating but it is now used very sparingly for transporting a small amount of oil, clay and goods traffic to the industrial estate at Heathfield.

The complete line from Moretonhampstead closed officially in 1959, but it was still retained for the delivery of goods traffic. This was in spite of efforts being made to persuade the company to reverse their decision to close the line when diesels began operating throughout British Rail. Finally, in 1964, the section above Bovey Tracey was finished even for freight, the rails being withdrawn from Bovey in 1971. The line closed after a special one-day service of passenger trains from Newton Abbot, put on especially for the enthusiasts.

Because of access to the track being restricted, if we want to keep as close as possible to the authentic route, we need to take the first left, after the track on the roundabout, along the old Newton Road. That is, of course, unless we use the Bovey Straight which, other than the pleasure of its overhanging trees, is likely to prove uninteresting as far as any link with the tramway is concerned.

The old Newton Road passes an industrial estate on the left and, as we approach Heathfield, we might turn into the first road on the left, taking us across the railway, thereby providing us with a view of the track on which the line was laid.

This road brings us out to School House, now renamed Little Bovey House,

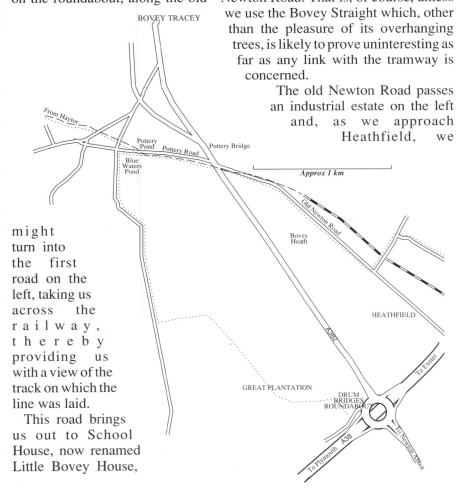

at the junction we would have reached had we taken the track from Pottery Bridge. At the School we could now turn right but, apart from the row of houses (Heathfield Cottages) leading to the railway, the road will only take us as far as the junction where the A.38 between Exeter and Plymouth crosses. Temporarily, this is as far as we can go in our search for the original tramway, for the A.38 is much too dangerous to attempt to cross at this spot. In order to explore the route further, we must return to Heathfield by retracing our steps and walking along Battle Road, meeting up with the Bovey Straight and on to the roundabout at Drum Bridges.

Regarding our alternative route, we need to return to Brimley to the point where we emerged from the bridlepath at Pottery Pond. This will take us through the more picturesque route, leading through the Great Plantation, for which our gratitude should be expressed to the Forestry Commission for the way they have so ably laid out the walk. Not that this is likely to remain a choice since an organisation known as Centre Parcs have recently acquired an option on the Plantation to turn it into a holiday resort with wooden chalets being strategically situated throughout the site. It is to be hoped that even if this should arise then the way through the Plantation will still be open, for if we fail to take advantage of this part of the walk, we would be denying ourselves one of the most enjoyable woodland rambles in the South West. Whilst strolling through the Plantation, which was part of the original Templer estate, it is easy to forget its proximity to the traffic roaring along the road.

The route is clearly way-marked, directing us to turn right from the bridlepath in Pottery Road, then turning left towards Liverton. Passing by houses on the left and a cul-de-sac on the right, we might look to the left to where the land has been reclaimed on the site of the Blue Water Mine, a large

pond now existing where the mine has been flooded. Progressing along this road we pass further signs on the right, identifying bridlepaths leading back to Chapple. About half a mile further on the Templer Way signs direct our steps into the Great Plantation, over a stile and along a laid out pathway. We can certainly appreciate how the Forestry workers have cleared the paths and constructed bridges and walkways over the muddier parts, trying to retain the natural character of the wood as closely as possible.

At any season of the year the walk is most exhilarating, but in summer or late spring nothing could surpass walking in solitude through such natural surroundings, allowing our minds to block out the cares of present day turmoil. Unfortunately, even though we are able to suppress the hum of the traffic from the A.38, we might be suddenly brought back to reality as a jet plane swoops low across the nearby heath. Yet, in spite of such infringements, we can concentrate on the walk itself and if we step stealthily we are likely to be well rewarded with the forms of wildlife inhabiting the site.

The call of many varieties of birds can be heard, and even the novice will experience little difficulty in differentiating between such birds as wood pigeon, magpie, jay or blackbird, besides the more melodious song-birds. We are also likely to hear, if not actually see, many of the birds whose habitat fluctuates between heathland, moorland and wood, including blue-tits, coal-tits, woodlarks, goldfinches, chaffinches, greenfinches, linnets and even woodpeckers.

In these days, when so much emphasis is put upon conservation, it is encouraging to hear success stories. In fact, it isn't unusual now to hear nightingales on the Bovey Heath. A report appeared in the *Mid Devon Advertiser* for June 23rd 1888 which read: "*The nightingale has this year been seen, though unfortunately not heard, in Devonshire, where on April 24th, a dead bird was picked up. The extreme rarity of the nightingale to the west of Exeter is a remarkable fact in the natural history of England.*" Such a report encourages us to believe that not all is being lost through modern developments.

During our ramble through the Plantation we will come across several patches of clearing where it might be advisable once again for us to keep a wary eye open for adders, which reportedly inhabit the wood in large numbers. This fact makes nonsense of a local legend which says that adders and wood ants do not make good neighbours, since the latter abound here in great profusion. Be that as it may, to pause and watch these miniature creatures performing their mundane tasks of building and searching for food, can indeed be fascinating.

The Plantation is also a haven for many other species of both common and rare insects plus moths and butterflies. Among those we are likely to see are yellow brimstones and perhaps the rare White Admiral, plus a variety of damsel flies. Much has also been written and spoken about one particular rare amphibian dwelling here in one of its few remaining habitats—the great crested newt, now a protected species.

Many of the larger mammals also make their home here and, even though they might rarely be seen, the evidence of their presence is clear. In spite of what some people might think, the signs warning the motorist that deer inhabit the wood are authentic, a fact which we had difficulty in accepting until we suddenly caught sight of a young doe peering out over the hedge in broad daylight, not more than thirty yards from where we were standing.

Besides the abundance of grey squirrels, other rodents such as stoats, and even mink—which escaped from farms—make their home in the Plantation.

Among the tasks performed by the Forestry workers has been the thinning out of much of the scrub in the more dense parts. Also the cutting back of the rhododendrons which, if allowed to spread at will, soon choke out the indigenous plants, some species of which are relatively rare. As we come towards the end of the track we are again conscious of how much work has been accomplished in making the walk accessible and pleasurable to all by the construction of bridges and platforms over the worst mud patches.

Crossing the final bridge and climbing the steps which have been built to take the walker up to the old A.38, we see the Templer Way signs directing

us around the top of the roundabout. Again it must be stressed how essential it is to take care for we have to cross at least three very busy roads. Therefore, any youngsters will need particular watching.

However, once we get on to the Newton Road, turning into Stover Park about twenty yards along, we can relax, perhaps making our way to the information-board to plan our next section of the walk.

No visitor to Stover Park could fail to be impressed with the way the site has been developed as a natural wildlife sanctuary which one is able to explore at

close quarters. Not that its potential is a recent discovery for, in his book on Devon, S. Baring Gould remarks how Stover Lake was: "In great request by skaters when sharp frosts allow for ice forming sufficiently strong to sustain them."

Such an invitation would hardly be recommended today, but it does help to highlight just how popular the area has been in times past.

Besides the walks around the lake, the waymarked Heritage Trails have been designed to include a visit to what remains of the canal at Ventiford, plus Teigngrace Village, together with its granite church—built in the period of Gothic revival—plus driveways to Stover House.

Approx 1 km

Heathfield

To Exeter

To Bovey Tracey

A38

DRUM BRIDGES ROUNDABOUT

To Plymouth

To Newton Abbot

Newpark Plantation

Car Park

STOVER LAKE

Ventiford Cottages

Templer Way

Heritage Trail

Stover House School

TEIGNGRACE

However, it is impossible to explore both the Templer Way and the Heritage Trails without retracing our steps in some parts. Therefore time spent planning the route will be rewarding.

Stover Park is becoming increasingly popular with tourists and locals alike, providing a place to relax in complete tranquillity, absorbing the peaceful environment away from the cares of everyday life.

As with the rest of the area covered by our walk thus far, many species of animal have made their home in the park, especially a wide variety of birds who find it to be a secure haven.

It has been claimed that enthusiasts have spotted almost 150 different types of bird here but, of course, those of us less experienced in ornithology could not expect to be so observant. Nevertheless, it might be an interesting exercise to see just how many species we are able to count and name.

An equal challenge might be to count the number of plants we are able to discover, besides the sedges and rushes which flourish on the marshlands around the lake. Some of the more common ones to look for might be the flag-iris, ragged robin, creeping forget-me-nots and Lady's smock, in early spring.

But no matter how limited our interest in such matters might be, meandering through the park, around the lake, is a step back into paradise, a haven and retreat from twentieth century problems.

The amenities provided in the park give us a chance to recuperate after our walk from Brimley and we might take advantage of the open picnic area which has been laid out near the car-park.

As noted on the information-board, the terrain varies from marshy ground surrounded by heathland scrub, and mixed woodland, intermingled with conifer plantations. Even before moving a step from this spot, we can cast our eyes around and recognise some of the more familiar trees. In front of us we can identify Scotch firs, Douglas firs and Tamarak trees, the cones of which are often to be found scattered all over the ground.

Proceeding along the pathway, our first sight of the lake can be quite impressive, with the waterlilies spread out across the lake like a multi-coloured blanket.

We won't be beside the water many seconds before we find ourselves surrounded by all manner of water-fowl: swans, coots, moorhens, and as many varieties of duck as we can name. Among these are the beautifully marked shelduck, busily searching the surface of the water for food. Some of these birds are so tame that they are prepared to feed from the hand. In fact, if one dares to ignore their demands they are likely to help themselves to any food which isn't kept under scrutiny. We might not be able to name many of the other birds we see further out on the lake, but we will easily recognise the many familiar types of gull, while on the marshes are several Canada Geese. Grebes are also fascinating to watch as they find sport in dipping and diving, providing us with much amusement as we try to guess where they will reappear after submerging.

To the left of the small observation jetty, from where we have been watching their antics, we cross a wooden bridge on the left, following the pathway around the perimeter of the lake. Paths also run alongside a stretch of water which was one of the feeders, taking us down almost as far as Drum Bridges.

As we retrace our steps around the perimeter, we might be glad of the opportunity of resting on one of the seats which have been strategically placed for us to observe other creatures who will soon appear when they consider it to be safe.

The walk along this northern edge brings us to a picturesque bridge crossing an overflow channel, on each side of which runs a path leading down to the Teigngrace Road.

From this bridge the track which we see going off to the left actually leads to the ruins of the granite lodge, lying adjacent to the A.380.

The banks of the overflow channel appear particularly inviting to the coots who favour nesting in the reeds on either side. At the far end of this channel we find yet a further rustic bridge which crosses the weir, from where the water trickles away into the old canal through various routes. At this spot the Templer Way signs direct us through a fairly thickly populated part of a wood where the pine needles lie on the ground like a thick pile carpet. After making our way through this labyrinth, we will find ourselves emerging on to the Teigngrace Road. Resisting for a moment the signs directing us along the small road on the opposite side, follow the road towards the hamlet of Ventiford, which is the point where the canal actually started. At the crossroads we pass a railway bridge on the left, then about twenty yards further along, beside the small cottage selling fresh produce, there is another bridge. Instead of following these signs for the Templer Way, continue towards Teigngrace where, just before arriving at the village, we will see more signs on the right, pointing the way up through two fields. The old gateway and iron fencing here were obviously once part of the perimeter and formed one of the entrances to Stover House. Now a modern gateway has been erected inside the old structure and forms part of the route of the Templer Way.

Strolling up through this path, it is interesting to notice the line of oak trees spreading across the fields, leading down to Teigngrace. They appear to be in such a symmetric line that it seems obvious that they were once part of the landscaping of the old house and grounds. Judging by their size though, this was most likely before the arrival of the Templer family, and it is practical to assume that it is from this line of trees that the farm 'Twelve Oaks', just beyond Teigngrace, got its name.

At the top of the pathway another gateway opens up in front of a small clay-pit, and here we are directed to the right along a further path through a wooded area. Here again a considerable amount of work has been done to make the walk more interesting, with many of the rhododendrons being cut back enabling new growth to establish itself.

At the top of this path we arrive at the rear entrance of Stover House which, because it now serves as a private school, is unfortunately not open for public viewing, although from time to time special arrangements are made for lectures regarding the history of the house.

Passing by the school, we see more of the original railings and fencing, whilst on the opposite side of the path stands an iron gatepost which is very pleasing to the eye. In spite of the workmanship which must have gone into producing such an object, it is sad to see that it now serves no other purpose than being a field gateway.

From here we have a pleasing view over meadows and woodland around Teigngrace and, as we pass the perimeter of the school, the route crosses a bridge over a dried out waterway, obviously once forming part of the lake's supply.

After this the road narrows into a track which eventually takes us back to the lower end of the lake, to the place where the bridge previously mentioned crosses the overflow channel, and we follow the route back to the car park.

BY CANAL OR RIVER TO TEIGN BRIDGE

If we are still keen to keep as close as we can to the tramway, we now need to make our way from Stover Park to Drum Bridges. From the top of this roundabout take the first turning to the right, walking along the grass verge on the south-bound carriageway of the A.38. Here again we must stress the need to watch for the traffic on this unpaved road.

Passing by the ruins of Stoford Lodge, turn right and proceed towards Teigngrace; about half a mile along we will come to the spot where we previously emerged from the walk around Stover grounds. This time, following the Templer Way signs opposite will take us across the railway track and down to Ventiford Cottages. The view from the top of the bridge will enlighten us as to what the journey must have been like for the teams of horses that pulled the trains down to the canal.

Ventiford Cottages were built to house the employees who worked on the railway and the canal; on the opposite side of the road we can see how the present enterprising occupants have found a quaint use for the old communal pump. The way they have bedecked it with plants not only adds colour to their environment but also helps to preserve it as a reminder of the harsh life-style endured by the previous occupiers. An inscription on the pump, 'Parker B. & Co., Newton', is no doubt a reference to the plumber of that name who lived in Courtenay Street, Newton Abbot at that time. At Ventiford Cottages the Templer Way leads back to the right towards Teigngrace Cross, but if we proceed about half a mile towards Brock Farm, we will find lying in the grass verge on the left side of the road, a granite slab which was clearly part of the tramway. Just why it happens to be lying here such a distance from the tramway is a bit of a mystery. However, it could be an encouragement for us to search for more relics of the industry which might still be found.

Retracing our steps past Ventiford Cottages will eventually bring us to the junction at Teigngrace Road, where we pass under the railway bridge. It has been said by some reports that many of the setts from the tramway were used in the bridge's construction, but this is obviously a confusion with the next bridge about twenty yards further along the track. This is found by walking along the road then turning left at the cottage advertising fresh produce for sale. The first bridge bears a plaque with the inscription: "The Horsehay Co. Ltd. 1934," indicating a much more recent innovation than when the line was first lain in 1866, whereas the granite setts already mentioned can be clearly seen in the second bridge.

The cottage beside this bridge was once occupied by the canal manager but the owners will now be only too pleased to supply such commodities as free-range eggs or cream, or perhaps provide us with some light refreshment.

The footpath under the bridge passes a wooden bridge on the left, opposite which we can see two gates leading into a small meadow. This was actually the start of the canal, forming the circular basin where the barges were loaded and turned.

Unfortunately the walker is restricted to keeping to the designated route along the banks of the River Teign, but it would be in one's interest to seek permission to search around here for the few remains of the

The Start of the Stover Canal

canal. Fragments of stone walls and the pillars of a gateway still exist as do many of the feeders into the canal.

During its lifetime, the canal was about two miles in length, consisting of five locks and two feeders, culminating in an overflow channel at Jetty Marsh. It is to be hoped that one day the walker will be permitted to walk the dried out bed of the canal, but sadly it is now too overgrown to allow access. However, in spite of this disappointment, the Templer Way walk has been so constructed to compensate our loss by running through beautiful scenery along the banks of the river, right down to Teign Bridge.

Many local people take advantage of strolling through these 'Teign Fields' where we might easily espy the quick flutter of a kingfisher among many other aquatic loving birds. The meadows are also particularly attractive to flocks of sandmartins which can be seen darting close over the ground, hungrily swooping on the insects which are disturbed, either by the cattle grazing, or the farm workers when the grass is mown. If we are making our walk in early summer, then the fields will be a picture as we observe the masses of buttercups and other meadow plants, often disturbed by the fresh earth of mole hills, the builders of which obviously thrive on the earthworms found in this rich soil which is susceptible to being flooded several times during the year.

Our journey leads us through a series of gateways across the meadows, but for this part of the walk we are only following the river bank as far as the signpost informing us that the Templer Way now divides and we have the choice of either making for Teign Bridge or Lock's Bridge.

Alternatively, if we were to cross the river by either of the two foot-bridges, we would find that the left path will take us to the village of Preston, whilst if we follow the path on the right we will eventually pass the clay-pits, meeting up with the road at Gallows Cross.

It might be appropriate here to mention an interesting discovery which was made in 1874. Within the clay workings, some twenty yards from the river, workmen found a bronze spear head. This was lying about twenty feet below the surface. This added to a previous find of a simply-carved, limbless, wooden figure with an extremely long neck, which caused much speculation about the previous habitation of the site.

However, instead of crossing the river, it might be appropriate to leave that part of the walk until later. Meanwhile, let us make our way to Lock's Bridge, which is accomplished by crossing the field to a wooden stile from where we cross yet another field to arrive at a narrow footbridge, through a hedgebank. This in turn leads through a five-bar gate, then over a footbridge, constructed from old railway sleepers.

Here we will notice a large stone slab lying beside the route. Although this doesn't appear to have any connection with the trade, the size of the stone does provide us with an idea of the type of cargo which was carried on the barges.

Arriving at Lock's Bridge Crossing, we can explore what is now possibly the best preserved lock on the whole system. It is quite interesting to see that water is still retained in the lock, even though most of the remainder of the canal ditch has long since dried out. Actually, it is claimed that this part of the canal has never been known to run dry, being fed by nearby streams seeping into it.

The walls of the lock were constructed from solid blocks of granite, with recesses on either side, which used to hold a pair of lock gates. Fortunately, there is a notice-board at this site to explain the manner in which the gates were operated. Apparently they worked in conjunction with a further pair of gates about 110 feet upstream, thereby allowing two barges at a time to pass through the system.

If we walk a short distance along the right hand path of the canal, we can still see the remains of the paddle gear at this top lock; then, by clambering down into the ditch we can examine the stone work at close quarters.

Across the railway track, stands a stone building—at present roofless—which also featured in the maintenance work which was performed on both the canal and the barges.

Going through the gateway across the track will bring us out to a small private road, passing by a house on the left, now called Teigngrace Manor. Details in the church tells us that this house played an important part in the conflict of the civil war of the seventeenth century.

From here, emerging on to the main road, a short turn to the left past the house called Grey Gables will bring us to the driveway to Teigngrace Halt, the platform of which we could just see from Lock's Bridge. Alternatively, turning left will give us an opportunity to spend time looking around the village of Teigngrace, paying particular attention to its church which was built by James Templer and his brothers, and where John Templer served as rector.

The church can be visited by first collecting the keys from one of the houses listed on the porch door but before we do, we might take particular note of the old oak tree growing at the side of the main road of the village. The girth of this tree will give us some indication of its age, suggesting that it has existed for centuries.

Walking up the pathway to the church, the first impression we receive is its 'olde worlde' effect which is rather out of place now among the modern bungalows that have sprung up around the village.

In front of the entrance stands a beautiful Yew tree which, judging by its height, was growing here before the present church was built. At the base of the tree is a seat, donated in 1957 in memory of a Mrs Caunter.

Teigngrace Church was built on the site of an earlier place of worship. Records of the vicars of Teigngrace dating back to 1350 are displayed just inside the porch. It is claimed that its history extends back to Saxon times, but the present church was built in 1787. It was originally constructed with a spire, and serves as an enduring memorial to the whole Templer family.

As we enter the church we see that the plaques around the walls are all dedicated to the various members of the family, and from these inscriptions we learn that their links with the East India Company were maintained by descendants of the family.

The plaques detail much of the history of the family, recording moments of tragedy such as when the youngest son was killed by shipwreck on 5th January 1786. The same applies in the case of a grandson who was also shipwrecked, dying at the premature age of twenty in November 1806.

The church itself is rather sparsely decorated but the altar piece is remarkable; painted by James Barry, it is a copy of Vandyk's 'Pieta' (the property of

Antwerp Museum).

After leaving the church we might continue our walk back towards Teignbridge to trace where the canal met up with Whitelake Channel. There are various routes we could take, such as turning left towards Newton Abbot, following the road past Whitehill, then turning first left after passing Sandford Orleigh into Jetty Marsh.

However, if we wish to continue following the line of the canal we need to retrace our steps back to Lock's Bridge.

Unfortunately we will not be able to walk along the derelict ditch since it again runs over private land where the walker is obliged to keep to the

established route. This means that we will be unable to explore Graving Dock Lock which lies about 440 yards downstream from Lock's Bridge. This is a pity for since the lock was functioning as recently as 1939, the locks and gates are in a fair state of preservation. Also nearby are the remains of a building which was used for steaming the timbers when the barges were under repair.

The area is now vastly overgrown, and even if the walker were permitted to visit the site they would find it an extremely arduous task. However, there is much talk at present of restoring the canal and it is hoped that this might be done whilst there are still artifacts worth saving.

Meanwhile, we have to content ourselves with pausing at Lock's Bridge, reflecting on what the journey must have been like during its hey-day. We can be grateful that the way has been opened for us to be able to continue our walk back along the river bank to Teignbridge, being fascinated with watching the water shimmering in the sunlight, maybe stepping on to some of the grassy islands which are plentiful. No wonder that during the summer months so many local people find it a favourite spot for swimming or sunbathing.

As we get to the end of the fields we might spend a little time admiring the bridge which carries what used to be the main road to Exeter. Reports tell us that when excavating the ground for dismantling and rebuilding this bridge in 1815, the timbers of an ancient wooden bridge were discovered, while underneath that were found the piers of yet another, apparently dating back to Roman times.

From here we reach the roadway by climbing steps, and we might turn left towards Gallows Cross to where we can take a pathway on the left around the perimeter of the ECC claypits. Until recent times Teignbridge House used to stand on this spot, but it was demolished to make way for the expansion of the clay workings.

According to the *Transactions of the Devonshire Association* for 1912, a work by J.T. Joyce records that: "Deep in the alluvium around [Teignbridge] lie foundations of many buildings indicating that there was once a considerable roadway settlement on either side of the river."

However, that was long before our ancestors realised the importance of the clay, excavating large caverns in their search for wealth. Actually, it is claimed that although the clay workings have already spread quite extensively in the area, there is still enough clay beneath the surface for the present supply to last another hundred years. However, it is to be hoped that not too many historical relics will have to be sacrificed in search of these minerals.

For the time being we can enjoy our stroll along the pathway, admiring the work which is carried out at the mine, picking our way through the path along the bank of the Teign. This will bring us back to the footbridge into Teign Fields and we can resume our journey along the Templer Way once more.

FROM TEIGN BRIDGE TO THE TEIGN ESTUARY

Having left the fields we emerge on to the main road at Teign Bridge and now have to make a further decision. As yet, there is no direct waymarked route from here until we again encounter the Templer Way signs at The Avenue in Newton Abbot. Therefore, we need to decide between turning left, then first right into Broadway Road through Kingsteignton or turning right, passing by Teignbridge Crossing, following the main road until we arrive at Jetty Marsh.

The fact that both routes contain interesting features appertaining to the clay trade and Templer's Way, makes it a difficult choice, but let's assume that we first decide to travel through Kingsteignton to investigate the remains of the Hackney Canal. Broadway Road will lead us right into Kingsteignton arriving at the crossroads known as the Fountain. Incidentally, the structure which gave its name to this crossroads, originally erected in 1887 by voluntary contributions, used to stand in the centre of the crossroads, but has now been relegated to a site at the side of the road, where it functions as a War Memorial.

Hackney Canal was dug because besides 'ball clay' being mined around Heathfield, it was also found on Lord Clifford's estates in Kingsteignton. Thus in 1843 he built the canal from Kingsteignton down to the north bank of the Teign. However, by 1928, as with the Stover Canal, this fell into disuse, and at present is little more than a heavily silted tributary of the Teign.

To reach Hackney Canal from The Fountain, we cross the roundabout into Church Road, walking past St Michael's Church, where the road merges into a footpath, just beyond the mill. This path will take us to Greenhill Way, past the depot of the South West Water Authority. Along this road, take the turning on the right leading to the Passage House Inn, an attractive public house which was erected in 1761, lying at the water's edge, an ideal stopping place for us to acquire some light refreshment.

The inn has recently undergone a great deal of development, now forming quite an impressive complex, but for the origins of this site we look to Roman times. It was here too that travellers from mediaeval times used to ford the river as they journeyed between Exeter and Torre Abbey, which means that even from that date it is likely that some form of inn existed as the travellers awaited the turn of the tide.

Certainly the breathtaking views up and down river are bound to impress us and, as we stroll along the pathway beside the canal, we will pass the ruins of several cottages which used to house the bargemen who operated on the canal and river. There are still residents of Newton Abbot and Kingsteignton who can lay claim to having been born in these cottages. Further along from these ruins we will see the remains of the wharf and basin, together with the original tidal lock and breakwater. Today this is about all that remains of Hackney Village, once quite a thriving little community.

Emphasising the important part played by the Clifford family in the clay trade, at least two of the barges operating out of Teignmouth were owned by Lord Clifford, therefore, although this canal was smaller than the Stover Canal, its prominence, in the industry, should not be overlooked.

Continuing to follow the pathway across open ground will return us to Greenhill Way, thence on to Kingsteignton to the Newton Road. On our way towards Newton Abbot we can see on the left the remains of the heavily buttressed clay cellars, now used as storehouses and warehouses for local industries.

Approaching Newton Abbot, we cross the River Teign, which at this point appears to be so narrow in comparison with the wide estuary such a short distance away. On the left of the road is the racecourse, behind which used to be the Hackney Marshalling Yards, once famous as being the largest railway goods yards south of Swindon.

During the time when the canals were the main form of transporting the clay, all this area was known as Newton Marshes, a name which is self-explanatory since during much of the year the nearby fields are waterlogged. Opposite the old goods yard we once again see the Templer Way signs directing down through the waste ground on the right, leading us towards the locks at Jetty Marsh. Here we will find many relics of the industry for it was here the canal ended by emptying into Whitelake Channel.

These lock walls are very well preserved and we are able to clearly discern the inscription, "George Templer Esq., 1824," a date which coincides with the period when he improved the estuary after he had acquired the contract for shipping the granite to London. Also we can see the mooring posts and other relics from the industry, making it an important stage in our walk in tracing its history; one which we certainly wouldn't want to miss.

Before making our way back to the Kingsteignton Road, it is also worthwhile spending some time investigating the plant life since much of the ground here has not been disturbed since the canal was functioning.

Arriving back at the top of The Avenue, we might be further interested in a pleasant diversion by turning into Jetty Marsh Road where, on the left, adjoining the farm buildings is a flight of eighty two steps leading up to Rundle Road. From here a pathway running along the top will provide us with a panoramic view of Kingsteignton and Hackney, plus Whitelake Channel from its start down to the junction with the River Teign. In the foreground we can clearly see the work which has recently been performed by the Water Authority in trying to improve the amenities along this section of waterway. In the eighteenth century, before this Channel was dug as a drain for Jetty

Marsh, and before its connection with the Stover Canal, the navigable Teign ended in what was, until recently, the site of the railway goods yard which we can now see in the foreground. On this site, was later erected yet another wharf at which the clay-barges were loaded.

It is possible that we might wish to retrace our steps by following this road from the top of the path, along Knowles Hill Road, onto the Bovey Road to pick up the route where we left it at Teignbridge Crossing. Here we can see many features which were connected with the canal. The bridge itself is of particular interest, being a single-span, stone and brick structure, built in 1798, and now providing us with an ideal observation point for gazing down into the dried-out ditch of the canal. However, it must again be repeated that the traffic is extremely heavy on this road, which was merely designed to carry horse-drawn vehicles, being barely wide enough to allow one car at a time to cross.

The bridge is a grade II listed structure on one side of which, under the keystone of the arch, can be seen the figure of a man's head, complemented on the other side by a goat's head, both of which can be inspected more clearly if we are prepared to climb down into the ditch. On the upper side of the canal we can see maintenance buildings, alongside which a lane runs parallel. This lane takes us upstream for about twenty yards to the remains of a further set of lock gates, now nothing more than a depression in the ground with a few ruins of the walls still in situ. Unfortunately this site again has been fenced off and is not accessible to the public.

On the opposite side of this road at Teignbridge Crossing lies another lane, flanked on one side by clay-cellars and the remains of the lock-keeper's cottage. These buildings all house small firms dealing in engineering and light industry or scrap metals

By 1866 this site at Teignbridge Crossing was the main wharf on the canal, but by that time it was only the section from here down which was in constant use. Upstream had become virtually obsolete and by 1887 had become overgrown and almost unnavigable, even though it still acted as one of the feeders into the canal.

Beside the crossing, running parallel to the track, is a lane, under the control of the Water Authority, which leads down to the junction of where the canal met up with Whitelake Channel at Jetty Marsh, but unfortunately this is not open to the public. This is a pity for it would link the whole route from

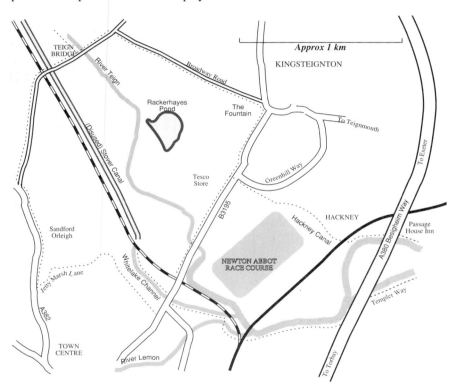

Ventiford to Teignmouth, taking the walker beside this marshland which again is a natural habitat for many unusual plants, besides the more common rushes, marsh-marigolds, comfrey and various reeds which in turn attract a wide variety of insects, butterflies and moths. Such conditions are an ideal environment for any budding entomologists who will be impressed with the claim that of the thirty seven species of dragonfly and damsel-fly known to breed in Britain, twenty four occur in the Bovey Basin.

The Whitelake Channel

The end of this lane opens out into a wide area which has been worked for its clay, but has now been reclaimed and it is hoped that one day it will be open to the public. Meanwhile, we have to content ourselves with following the metalled road from Teignbridge Crossing back to Newton Abbot. Just beyond the crossing we pass over an extended bridge over an expanse of marshy ground, which again provides an opportunity to be conscious of the environment. In the adjoining fields, which are often flooded, can be seen Canada Geese, and we might catch sight of the occasional heron stalking fish or eels. We might also take a moment to pause on the bridge to notice what attracts such birds. When the fields are in flood, shoals of small fish can be seen darting in and out of the grasses. Passing further along this road, past the turn-off to Teigngrace on the right, we come to a lone house, together with the ruins of barns. Within living memory this used to be a poultry farm but the outbuildings now seem to be falling into disrepair.

This is an important bit of roadway, for in the previously quoted *Transactions of the Devonshire Association*, J.T. Joyce tells us how it is most likely that the road to Newton from Exeter used to run along here, meeting up with the top of Jetty Marsh, rather than its present route over the top of Whitehill. Again, upon approaching Whitehill Garage on the Newton-Bovey Road, we must stress the need for caution for neither side of the road is paved.

As we climb Whitehill we pass on the right a pathway leading to Highweek Church, while on the left of the road is the entrance to Sandford Orleigh, the home George Templer built for himself when his fortunes changed, after his parting with Stover estate to the Duke of Somerset.

From here the next turning on the left is Jetty Marsh Lane, another example

An old aerial view of the area near the former Power Station

of an old English country lane which has remained undisturbed by modern agricultural methods. This is also a private road which, although now open to the public, used to be closed to the public once a year in order to establish its owner's rights. Even so, it seems that there will soon be dramatic changes here for this is planned to feature greatly in the town's redevelopment scheme.

Halfway along, this lane veers to the right where there is a small quarry which, like others in the area, was worked for its limestone for local use. On the opposite side of the road is an old building, which at one time was used in the cider industry. This area has now been fenced off from the public, but a small lock basin used to exist here before it was removed when the land was reclaimed. Actually, on the far side of this piece of open ground is the lock where the canal emptied into the Whitelake Channel and where we would have emerged if we had been permitted to use the lane from Teignbridge Crossing.

However, no matter how we arrive at this point at the junction of Jetty Marsh Lane with Kingsteignton Road, we are now ready to make the final leg of the journey, following the river to Teignmouth.

ALONG THE ESTUARY TO TEIGNMOUTH

The organised walks along the Teign Estuary usually start at the quay at the bottom of Forde Road. However, there is good reason for us to consider starting from the roundabout at the top of The Avenue on the Kingsteignton Road, for there are many interesting features to be observed before we arrive at the wharf.

On The Avenue side of the Kingsteignton Road, a gateway beside the National Tyre Services depot will take us along the banks of the lower part of Whitelake Channel, giving us the opportunity to catch sight of many more small birds, including kingfishers. At the end of this pathway the council have recently laid out a picnic area, making the route even more attractive. In fact, if we keep to this path, going under the rail bridge, it will allow us to see where the Channel empties into the Teign and if we struggle through the marshy ground here we can search for more unusual plants and insects.

However, it may be that instead of joining this path from the top of The Avenue we might decide to keep to the roadway as far as Wharf Road. This would give us a chance to see other industrial sites which had links with the river, without our having to deviate from the route very much. The first example of this can be seen just about twenty yards along The Avenue where we find the road crossing what remains of the Leat, a stretch of water flowing from Bradley down through the town, which used to supply all the mills on its way before running into Whitelake Channel. Alongside the forecourt of Renwick's Car Showrooms we can still see the last of these mills, the Bark Mill, which used to feature prominently in the tanning of the leather from

Bradley Tan Yards.

About thirty yards further on, we come to Wharf Road, but before we continue along here, we might turn into Marsh Road, on the opposite side, and about a hundred yards along this road we will notice a slipway leading down to the River Lemon. This was previously used by the market boats for unloading passengers who came up the river from Teignmouth and Coombe Cellars.

Besides passengers there were also boats which brought cargoes of wood up to the timber yards, which existed not only on the river itself, such as the one on the site of the power station, now in its turn also demolished, but also on what is now the centre of Newton Abbot, roughly the area now being the market precinct.

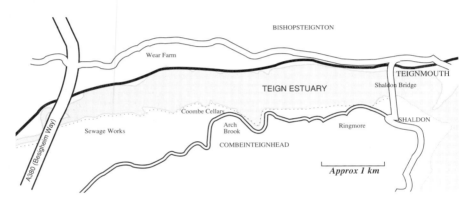

However, to continue our walk, let's return to The Avenue and cross the road into Wharf Road, which as its name suggests, used to extend down to the water's edge and where, at least until the 1950s, dredging used to be carried on.

It is interesting to talk to men who worked on this task, such men as Mr Bill Lang who was employed in the industry in the 1920s. We couldn't help but be impressed to hear of the changes which have been made since that time; to hear of the interesting experiences of how several people have been drowned in the river at one time or another, some deliberately, some accidentally. These old hands can also provide such details as how the men who punted the barges along the river very soon developed a permanent yellow bruising on their shoulders and chests where they applied their weight to the poles.

Meanwhile, to make our walk more interesting, we might notice that half-way along Wharf Road, a narrow lane is signposted as Templer Way, leading down beside the river, across which we can see the aptly-named new estate of Templer's Way, built on the site of the old power station. Evidence of this

previous occupier is easily identified by the existence of outfall pipes which used to return the water to the river after it had been through the cooling tower, for many years a prominent landmark of Newton Abbot.

On this part of the walk we need to be nimble-footed, for the way of crossing the river is by means of an iron bridge, which can be rather precarious in wet weather. Even so, it is relaxing to pause on top of the bridge to peer into the water in the hopes of sighting trout or mullet who might have escaped the bills of cormorants or herons who fish at the spot where the waters meet. If we approach the site cautiously we are likely to encounter either of these birds, and on most days as many as twenty or more swans can also be seen here.

For those who would find the iron bridge hazardous it is just as easy to turn into Templer's Way from The Avenue and follow the tow-path on the south side of the river; either route bringing us to the railway bridge at the bottom of Teign Road.

"... the cooling tower, for many years a prominent landmark of Newton Abbot."

Once again this could provide us with a little deviation for, by turning into Teign Road, we see the buildings of Tucker's Mills and Malt Stores, established by Edwin Tucker and built in 1900. This has added to the amenities provided for the visitor in that tours are now arranged around the mill in order to see how the barley was turned into malt for supplying the various breweries. Besides having the process explained, the visitor is encouraged to experience turning the barley themselves, then to taste the finished product. After this very interesting guided tour one is able to fortify oneself at the cafe before resuming the walk to Teignmouth.

At the quay we notice that a great deal of effort has been put in to developing the site as a recreational area and it is hoped that this work will continue. The old mooring posts remain, as does the plinth on which once stood a capstan, used in the loading and the turning of the tugs and barges. No doubt we will be pleased to see how the base of this capstan has been utilised as a feature of the quay, thereby adding further to its chances of being preserved.

A further point of interest here is that when the power station was in existence, there used to be another bridge at this spot, leading across to a pump house situated on the opposite bank. The base of the ladder to this bridge can still be seen on one of the mooring posts. Around the site seats have been erected to enable the traveller to relax, spending a few moments enjoying the scenery, perhaps watching the locals fishing from the banks. There is certainly a great deal of scope for this area to be developed further, to attract resident and visitor alike.

Leaving the wharf and continuing our walk, the way-marked signs direct us into the bottom of Forde Road, past the old Railway Coal Yard, now occupied by Teignbridge Propellers and, turning left past Graham's builders' yard and

J.R. Cull, we come to a path at the end of the road leading over more reclaimed land. From this path we cross a small footbridge over the Aller Brook, another favourite spot for swans who spend hours patiently searching for anything edible coming floating down through the brook.

The route now takes us away from the built-up section of the walk, and it is exhilarating to see the river stretching out before us, all the way to Teignmouth. It is doubtful whether this view differs very much from that seen by those men who propelled the flat-bottomed barges, with their cargoes of clay or granite, over a century ago. As one looks across the water, it seems only natural to expect to see one of those old tugs, even now chugging downstream with its line of barges in tow.

From here, down to Arch Brook, the walk along the footpath is clearly defined, keeping to the foreshore, except for a small detour which, depending

An old view of Teign fishermen

on the tide, we might find it necessary to make around Netherton Point.

Nevertheless a further note of caution must be expressed about this section of the walk, for not only should we check the tide times, but when venturing along the shoreline, we must be wearing suitable footwear. The importance of this will soon be verified as we are picking our way over rocks or squelching through muddy sections. These stones and sand can be quite sharp, and in certain places very slippery, particularly when the river is 'dirtier' than normal, that is, when throwing up a mass of seaweed.

As we pass under the bridge of the dual carriageway, we might be surprised by the extent of its span. Although only four pillars actually carry the bridge over the river, a further sixteen are required to stretch across the marshes to Hackney.

Looking across the river, we get a good view of the Passage House Inn, plus the ruins of the bargemen's cottages. Journeying further downstream we will certainly be impressed by the varieties of butterflies flitting among the nettles and other foliage. These range from Small-browns, Small-whites, Fritillaries, Peacocks and even Red Admirals, a definite must for those interested in Lepidoptera. Obviously the oak trees, nettles and bushes beside the track provide ample food and shelter for these and the great variety of other insects found there, enticing the most inexperienced of us to try to see how many we can name.

A short distance from the bridge we pass the sewage works and, looking out across the river, we see how the marshlands are a haven for a variety of sea-birds. No doubt we will be able to discern the different waders, and we will certainly have no difficulty in recognising the cormorants, standing on mooring buoys, with their outstretched wings, looking for all the world like little old men performing physical exercise.

The trip along the river is over four miles in length, but if we decide that the whole journey is too much, we might detour up the small track leading towards Buckland Barton. This is situated a little further on from the sewage works but we will need to look carefully for the entrance since it is rather overgrown.

Bear in mind that since we are not able to cross the dual carriageway, this will be our last chance to return to Newton Abbot until we have completed the journey to Teignmouth. It is possible to terminate the walk at Coombe Cellars and walk back along the B.3195, but this would be very dangerous since it is a very narrow unpaved road.

If we are making our walk sometime between the dates of 15th March and 15th September, we might be fortunate encough to come across a group of fishermen, busily netting salmon, following the tradition of their forefathers of many generations, using more or less the same techniques. Not that this always proves to be a lucrative trade, but apparently, along with raking for cockles, the cultivating of mussels and oysters, plus supplementing their incomes with boat trip for the tourists, most of the men in the work say that they manage to eke out a living.

As we approach the area bordered by Netherton Woods, we can be thankful that we took note of the tides, for the water level temporarily cuts off this part of the foreshore daily, forcing one to climb the steep wooded banks to meet up with the footpath in the adjoining field leading from Netherton House to Coombe Cellars. Netherton Woods is a favourite nesting site for the colonies of herons inhabiting the river, and it can be quite a challenge to see how near we can approach these relatively timid birds before they take flight.

After passing the woods, whether along the foreshore or by means of the footpath, we arrive at the Victorian inn of Coombe Cellars, the haunt of the boating and sailing fraternity.

Outside the inn is yet another Templer Way notice-board; this one informs us that the inn was once frequented by smugglers. It also tells us that in the days before the river was dredged, the existence of a lot more silt in the river meant that it was possible to cross from one side to the other on horseback. There is also a suggestion that an underground passage to the other side once existed. This might seem a little hard to accept until one is prepared to move some distance away from the area and note how the site on which the inn stands, juts out some distance into the river, which causes one to wonder whether such a legend could be a possibility.

Whether there is any truth in the further statement that it was also a clandestine meeting place for Lord Nelson and Emma Hamilton, we leave to the more romantically minded to dwell upon, however, there is no denying that the whole area is one of great scenic beauty; a perfect trysting place for lovers. While at Coombe Cellars, we are brought face to face with so many modern types of recreation such as sailing and rowing. In recent times much of the adjoining land has been taken over by caravans and other forms of camping, all very much pandering to the needs of the tourist. This is an ideal spot for some light refreshment before negotiating the final part of the journey. If, when we leave Coombe Cellars, the tide is too high to allow us to continue walking over the foreshore, we can climb over a stile, through a gate about fifty yards along the path at the bottom of the playing field, and from here return to the walk along the river once again.

Following the course of the river to Arch Brook, we can investigate what is

thought to be the remains of the last of the clay barges which were used on the river. This claim has been disputed by some, but certainly this relic seems to fit the characteristics of the barges. We might wonder why the wreck has been allowed to rot away in such a manner, but of course it brings to mind that traditionally the fate of all boats was that they should not be burnt or destroyed but just allowed to disintegrate.

Unfortunately, from here to Shaldon, there is no public footpath, and although it is possible to walk along the B.3195, this is certainly not recommended for walkers under any circumstances.

Consequently, it is best to try to choose a time when we can pick our way along the whole foreshore to Shaldon, where we can cross the road bridge to Teignmouth, making our way to the 'New Quay' built by Templer with the same Haytor granite, and thus to the conclusion of our trip.